PLAY LEAD GUITAR TODAY!

BEGINNING LEAD GUITAR

BY RON CENTOLA

To Jennifer and Mark

Technical Photos by Ron Centola

Edited by Anna H. Centola and Gary Centola

Creative photography by Rodman Wesley Benedict

TABLE OF CONTENTS

GENERAL INTRODUCTION 4

PHOTO CHART 5

FINGERING 6

COUNTING 7

WHAT'S NEXT? 8

THE SLIDE 10

    Bass Slide 12

    Echo Slide 13

    Last Slide 14

THE BEND 15

    Bending Notes 16

    Simple Bend 17

    Double Bend 18

    Bending and Double Picking 19

    Bend and Slide 20

THE HAMMER 22

HAMMER, BEND, AND SLIDE 26

DOUBLE NOTES 27

    Double Notes And A Hammer 29

    Bending Double Notes 30

COMPLETE LEAD - NUMBER ONE 31

    Part I 31

    Part II 32

    Part III 33

    All Parts 34

    Photo Charts 35

COMPLETE LEAD - NUMBER TWO 36

    Part I 36

    Part II 37

    Part III 38

    Part IV 39

    All Parts 40

WRITE YOUR OWN LEAD 42

COMPLETE LEAD - NUMBER THREE 43

    Part I 43

    Part II 44

    Part III 45

    All Parts 46

NOTE AND GUITAR POSITION GUIDE 48

GENERAL INTRODUCTION

It is my intention, through this book, to give the guitarist a real opportunity to learn how to play lead guitar. A lead is the solo guitar part in a song. I have worked out some leads and placed them on a Photo Chart, which I developed to help the guitarist who has problems reading music. By using the Photo Chart you can actually see what the leads look like on the neck of the guitar. By using this method you will soon be able to play leads you never thought you were able to play.

Ron Centola

THE PHOTO CHART

Photo Chart

1) The **Photo Chart shows** you the **string** and **fret position** of **each note** in the lead.
2) At a glance the **Photo Chart** will show you what the entire **lead looks like on the neck** of the **guitar.**

The string and fret position of the notes below are shown on the Photo Chart by the number directly above them as shown by **note 4.** *The symbol placed next to* **note 4** *is a # (sharp) sign. You don't have to worry about the # (sharp) sign because we have already sharped the note's position on the Photo Chart. The position of the sharped note 4 would be as shown on Photo Chart.*

How to Follow the Photo Chart

1) The **number in the oval above the note** will **correspond** with the **number in the oval** on the neck of the guitar **in the Photo Chart.**
2) The **frets have been numbered** on the Photo Chart so that you may find the fret position more quickly on your own guitar.

The notes above are played on the string and fret positions as written below:

Note ①　String 1　Fret 10
Note ②　String 2　Fret 6

Note ③　String 4　Fret 8
Note ④　String 5　Fret 4

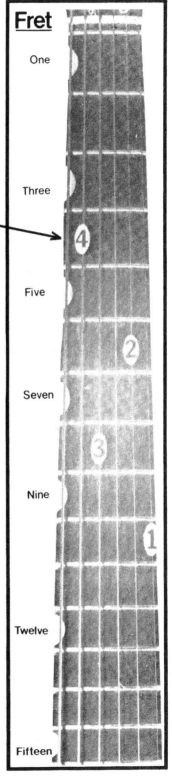

FINGERING

In order to move from note to note with the greatest ease, you must use the correct fingering technique.

How The Finger Guide Works

As you saw on the previous page, the number in the oval represents the note below it. The same is true with the Finger Guide. The **number in the oval** is **next to the finger** that **you use to play the note.** Look at the example below.

Example

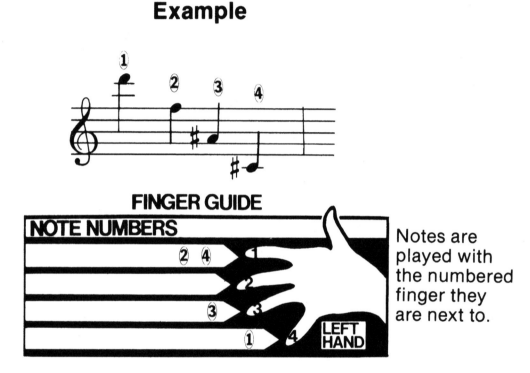

FINGER GUIDE

Notes are played with the numbered finger they are next to.

*Notes are represented on this guide by the number in the oval directly above them.

By using the Finger Guide above you can see that **notes ④ and ② are played with finger 1. Note ③** is played with **finger 3. Note ①** is played with **finger 4.**

COUNTING

BEAT- A beat is a duration of time. A beat is equal to the time it takes to tap your foot. The down up motion of your foot equals ONE beat. Beats would vary in time with the speed you tap your foot.

Counting Guide

NOTE/REST NAME	NOTE/REST FORM	TIME DURATION	HOW TO PLAY
Triplet		1 Beat	You should be able to play all three notes in a triplet in one Beat or one tap of your foot.
Eighth Note		½ Beat	Speed these notes up.
Quarter Note		1 Beat	Strike the note and proceed to the next note.
Dotted Quarter Note		1½ Beats	Strike the note and count ½ Beat before proceeding to the next note.
Half Note		2 Beats	Strike the note and count 1 Beat
Dotted Half Note		3 Beats	Strike the note and count 2 Beats
Whole Note		4 Beats	Strike the note and count 3 Beats
Eighth Rest		½ Beat	½ Beat of silence
Quarter Rest		1 Beat	1 Beat of silence
Half Rest		2 Beats	2 Beats of silence
Whole Rest		4 Beats	4 Beats of silence

1) An eighth note by itself looks like ♪. When two eighth notes are together they are connected with a straight line ♫ .

2) The **direction** of the **stem does not affect** the **beat value** of the note.

WHAT'S NEXT?

This book has been divided into five parts. First it deals with four basic techniques or components of playing lead guitar. The four techniques dealt with are: the slide, the bend, the hammer, and the double note.

After each technique is explained, a "mini-lead" using that technique is set out so you can practice the technique you have just learned. These leads are graded in difficulty.

After all four techniques are presented, "complete" leads are broken down into parts. You should practice and perfect each part of the complete lead. Once you have perfected each part, you can combine the parts for a truly great lead.

THE SLIDE

A **slide** is the **sound created** by **striking a note** with **a pick** and then **sliding your finger** from **that note** to the **next note**. The symbol used for a slide will be a arrow ➝. The **arrow** will be placed directly **under** the **note it affects**.

Photo Chart

Lead (Example of a Slide)

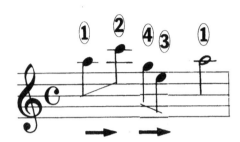

Special Instructions

In the lead written above, strike **note** ① and then, while holding down your finger on **note** ①, slide up the string to **note** ②. Stopping the slide on **note** ② will create the desired sound. (**Note** ① is on **string 1, fret 5. Note** ② is on **string 1, fret 8. This is shown on the Photo Chart.**) The striking of **note** ②, once you reach it, is optional. You use the same procedure to slide from **note** ④ to **note** ③, except you are sliding down the neck on **string 2**.

Counting

Notes ① and ②, **notes** ④ and ③, are eighth notes. You should be able to play **note** ① and ② in one beat, or one tap of your foot. You should also be able to play **notes** ③ and ④ in one beat or one tap of the foot. The time it takes to slide from one note to another is considered part of the total value of the notes. In other words, to slide from **note** ① to ② takes one beat.

Fingering

If you are playing **note** ① with **finger 1**, you could slide **finger 1** to **note** ② or you could strike **note** ② (with **finger 3.** You may use fingering that is comfortable to you as long as you complete the slide in the proper amount of beats.

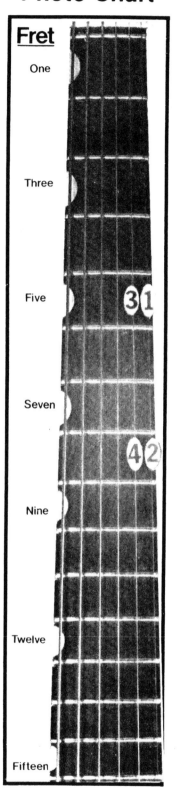

THE SLIDE

Photo Chart

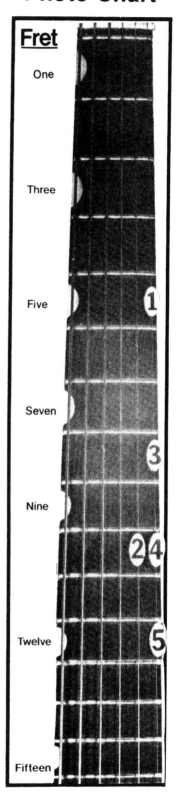

Special Instructions

When you see the **symbol ⊓**, **pick the string down** (strike the string in a downward motion with your pick.) When you see the **symbol ∨**, **pick the string up.**

You should pick **notes ②** with a quick, down-up movement. **Notes ②** are **eighth notes,** so you should be able to **pick both notes in one beat.**

After you pick note ①, slide to **note ②, string 2, fret 10** from anywhere below the note. In other words, you could start your slide to **note ②** from **fret 10,** or **fret 9,** or **fret 7,** etc.

Don't forget to slide from **note ⑤** to **note ④**.

Counting

Notes ① ③, ④, are used as **quarter notes. You play them** and **proceed to the next note.** They are worth one beat. **Notes ②, ③, ④,** are used as eighth notes. Remember you can recognize **eighth notes** because they are **tied with a straight line ♫ .** The two **eighth notes** should be **played in one beat. Note ⑤** is a **half note** and is **worth two beats.** Strike **note ⑤** and then count one beat. Refer to your Counting Guide on page 7.

FINGER GUIDE

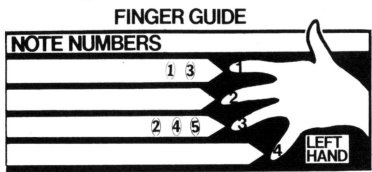

Bass Slide

A bass slide is a slide that is played on the **bass strings,** or the 3rd, 4th, 5th, and 6th strings.

Photo Chart

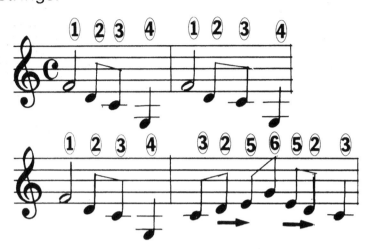

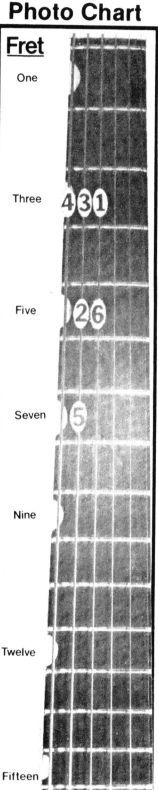

Counting

You can save yourself a lot of trouble and confusion if you memorize the note values on the Counting Guide on page 7. There are three kinds of notes in the leads written above. There are **half notes** which are worth **two beats.** There are **quarter notes** which are worth **one beat.** There are **eighth notes** which are **played faster** since **two eighth notes equal one beat.**

FINGER GUIDE

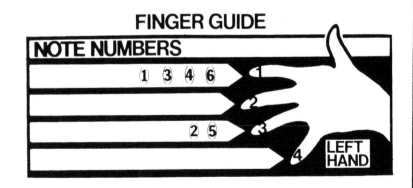

Echo Slide

This is called an **echo slide** because the lead is played on the **higher sounding strings** (strings 1, 2) and **repeated on the lower strings,** (strings 5, 6).

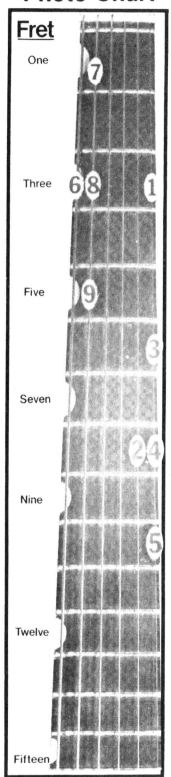

Special Instructions

Remember you should use the Photo Chart to locate the position of the note on the neck of the guitar. However, to look back and forth from the notes to the Photo Chart for every note can be confusing and aggravating. In order to avoid this confusion, you should **memorize the position** of **the note on the guitar. Note** ① is used two times in this lead. Look at **Note** ① and **try to remember** that it is on **string 1, fret 3.** If you can **remember** the **position of note** ①, you **won't have to look** at the **Photo Chart when it appears again** in the lead. **Use the same process for the rest of the notes.**

FINGER GUIDE

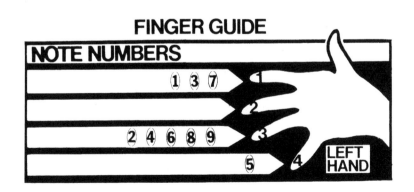

Last Slide

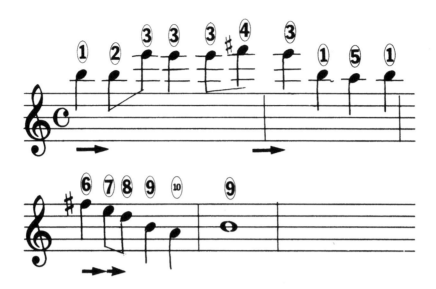

Special Instructions

This lead uses most of the neck of the guitar. (Look at the Photo Chart.) Don't get discouraged, it takes a lot of practice in order to master moving up and down the neck of the guitar smoothly. This **entire lead should take** only **sixteen beats** or **sixteen taps** of **your foot**.

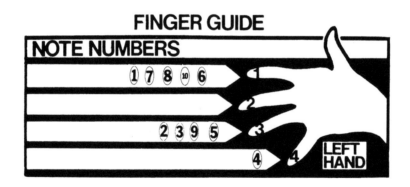

Photo Chart

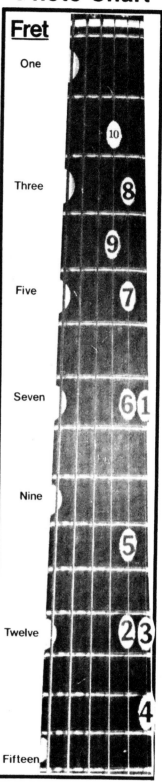

THE BEND

Bending Notes

Photo Chart

Bending a note refers to the technique that **creates the sound** used in many leads by **pushing** or **pulling** on **the note.**

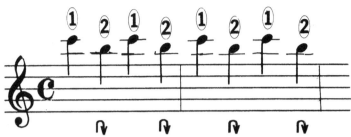

The **symbol** for **bending a note** will be ⋔

Special Instructions

Under **note 2** you can see the symbol for bending the **note.** To bend **note 2** press on **string 2, fret 12** and strike the second string with your pick. After you pick the second string, push **note 2** toward the third string. This will create the bending sound.

Counting Review

The bending of a note must be done in time. In other words, the **lead written** above must be done **in eight beats.**

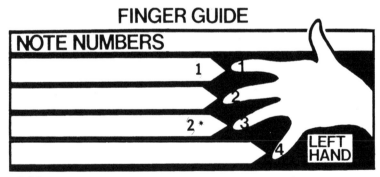

FINGER GUIDE

NOTE NUMBERS

1

2 *

LEFT HAND

* You may use your fourth finger.

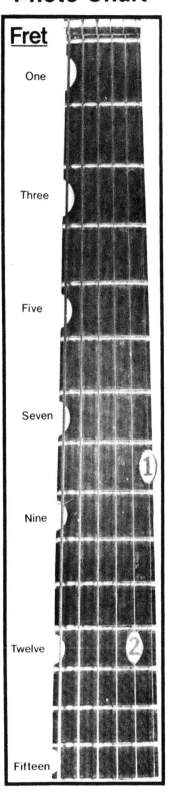

Fret

One

Three

Five

Seven

Nine

Twelve

Fifteen

Simple Bend

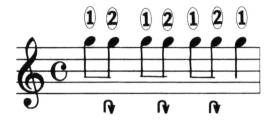

Special Instructions

You will have to practice going from **note** ① to **note** ② on **string 2, fret 8.** You must bend **note** ② and then immediately go back to **note** ①. You must do this in one tap of your foot.

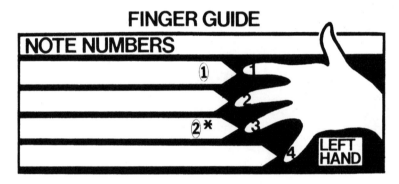

* You may want to practice using your fourth finger.

Student Notes

Photo Chart

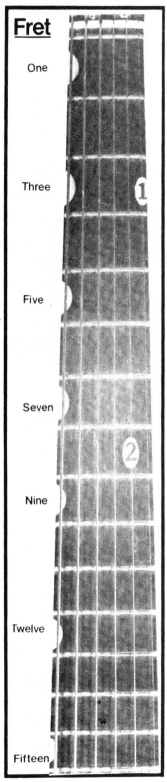

Double Bend

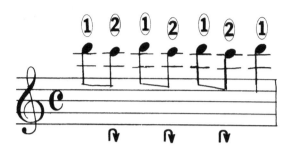

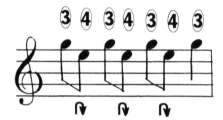

Special Instructions

In order for your leads to really sound nice you must be able to **move up and down the neck of the guitar quickly and smoothly.** You should be able to play this lead within the count of the eight beats.

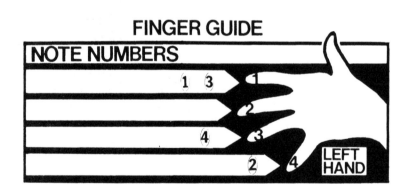

Photo Chart

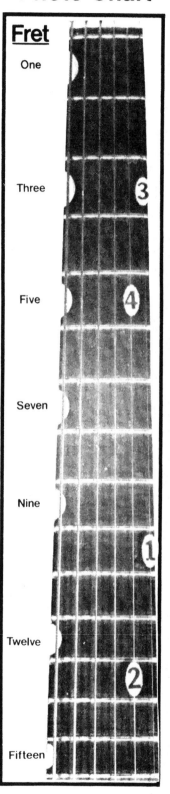

Bending And Double Picking

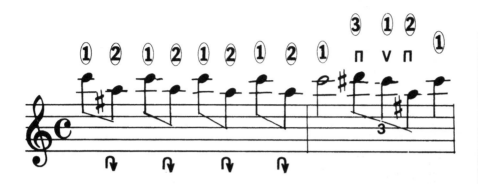

Photo Chart

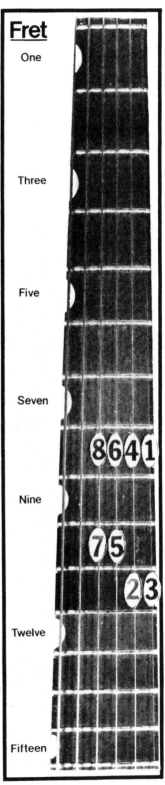

Special Instructions

This lead involves the bending and double picking of notes. **Notes ③, ①, ②**, and **notes ⑤, ⑥,** must be played smoothly in the flow with the lead.

Counting Review

Notes ③, ① ②, form a triplet. In a **triplet** all **three notes** should be **played in one beat. Notes ⑤, ⑥** are **eighth notes** and also should be played in one beat.

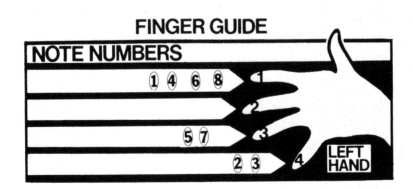

Bend And Slide

We will **combine** the **bend** and **slide techniques** in this lead.

Special Instructions

You should be able to play this lead in **eight beats**. The symbols for the bends and slides will be placed directly below the notes that are affected.

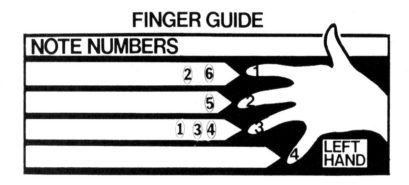

Student Notes

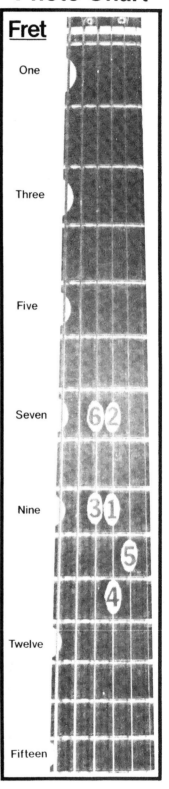

Photo Chart

THE HAMMER

The **hammer sound** is used in many leads. This sound is **created** by the **striking of the finger** of the **left hand on a note.**

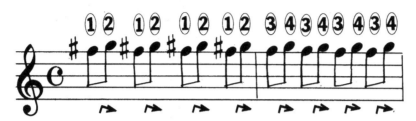

Special Instructions
The Left Hand

The **symbol** for the **hammer** will be ⌃ . It will be placed directly under the note it affects. The **hammering sound** is **created** by **striking the note** on the neck of the guitar **with the fingers of your left hand.** In the lead given above, you should play **note** ① with your **second finger** and then **slam** your **third finger down** on **note** ② to **create** the **hammer sound.** It is very important that you **leave** your **second finger** on **note** ① as you **hammer** or **slam note** ② with your **third finger.** (You should use the **same process** for **hammering note** ④.)

The Right Hand

Pick **note** ① with your right hand. You don't have to pick **note** ② because **note** ② will be sounded by the hammering of it by finger three.

Counting

The hammering must be done within the time allowed the hammered note. In other words, the **lead** given **above** would have to be **played** in **eight beats**.

FINGER GUIDE

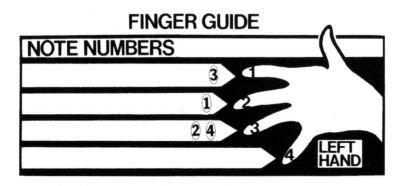

Photo Chart

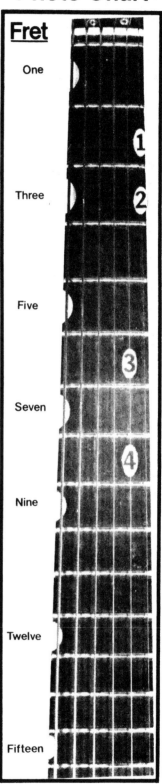

Hammer (con't.)

Special Instructions

While playing **this lead** you will be **hammering with** your **third finger.** Remember to hold your first finger down as you hammer with your third finger.

Counting Review

Do not pause between the three sets of triplets. Each set of triplets should take one beat. **This lead should be completed in four beats.**

FINGER GUIDE

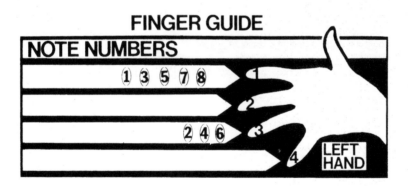

Student   Notes

Photo Chart

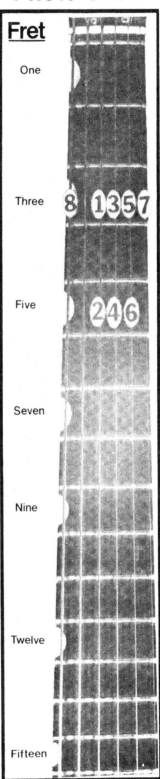

Hammer (con't.)

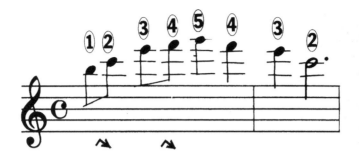

Special Instructions

You should use your **second finger** to do the **hammering in this lead.** Remember to **hold your first finger** down as **you hammer** with **your second finger.**

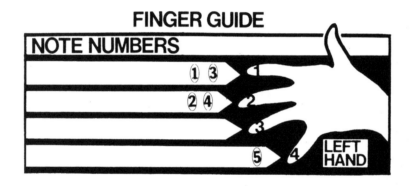

Student Notes

Photo Chart

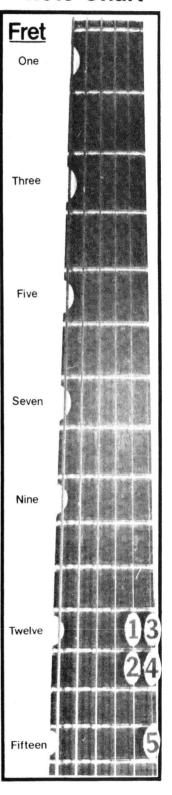

Hammer (con't.)

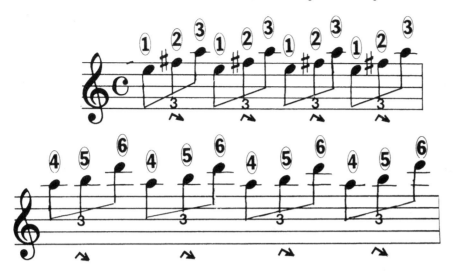

Special Instructions

While playing this lead you should be **hammering with** your **third finger.** You must be able to **move** from **fret 5** to **fret 10 smoothly** and without breaking time.

Counting Review

All these sets of notes are triplets. This entire **lead** should be played in **eight counts.**

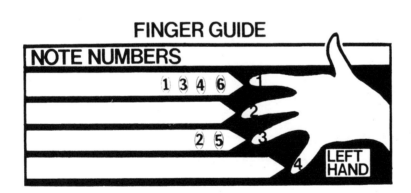

FINGER GUIDE

Photo Chart

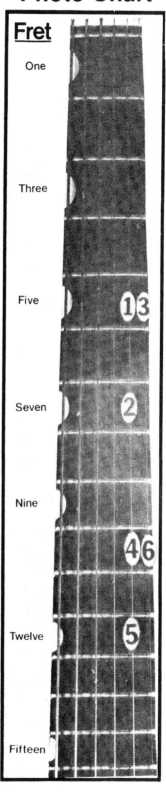

HAMMER, BEND, AND SLIDE

Photo Chart

While playing the following lead you will employ all three techniques you have learned; the bend, the slide, and the hammer.

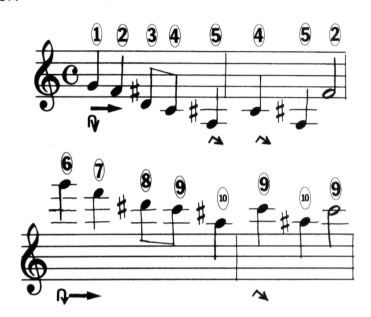

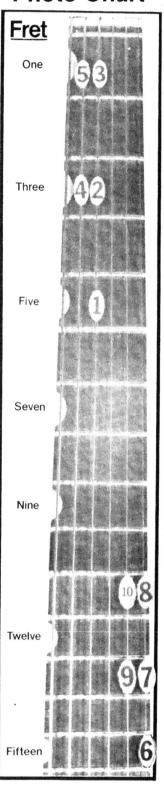

Special Instructions

On the top part of the lead you should bend note ①. Then you must slide from **note** ① to **note** ②. You must then **hammer note** ⑤.

FINGER GUIDE

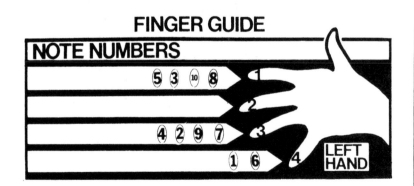

DOUBLE NOTES

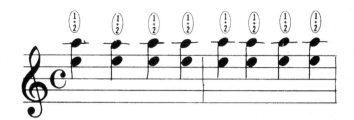

Photo Chart

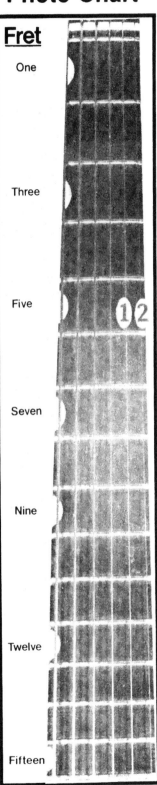

Fret

One

Three

Five

Seven

Nine

Twelve

Fifteen

Special Instructions

Double notes are **combinations of notes** that should be **played** at the **same time.** In the lead written above you should simultaneously **play notes** 1 and 2 as seen on the Photo Chart. Since **both notes** are on the same fret and next to each other, you can play them both with your first finger. To play these double notes you should **strike both strings at the same time.**

Counting Review

Double notes have the **same time value** as if they **were a single note.** In the lead given above, each double note is worth one beat. Refer to note values on page **7.**

FINGER GUIDE

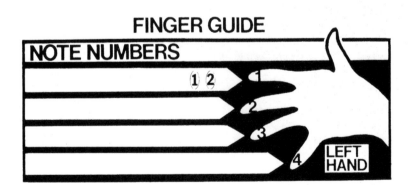

NOTE NUMBERS

1 2

1
2
3
4

LEFT HAND

Double Notes (con't.)

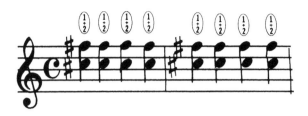

Special Instructions

The double notes in the lead above have to be played with two different fingers because the two notes used in these double notes are on different frets. You should **use** your **second** and **third fingers to play** these **double notes.** Remember, you have to **strike the second** and **third string** at the **same time.**

Counting Review

Each of the double notes above is worth one beat because they are quarter notes. You should **play the lead** in **eight beats.**

FINGER GUIDE

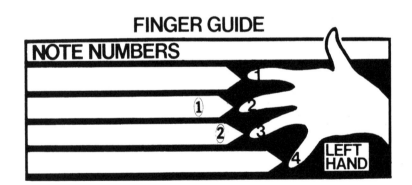

Photo Chart

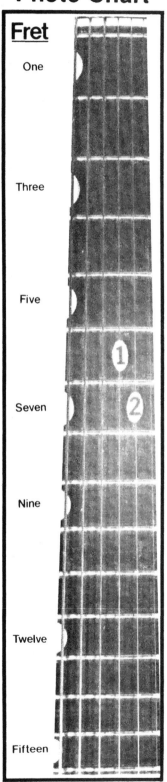

Double Notes And A Hammer

Special Instructions

In order for your lead to sound right you must be able to play the double notes quickly and smoothly. It may help to try to **place both fingers down** on the double notes **at the same time.** In other words, while playing those double notes consisting of **notes** ③ and ④ you should try to place your second finger on **note** ③ at the same time that you are placing your third finger on **note** ④. This will take a great deal of practice but it really is the key to playing double notes.

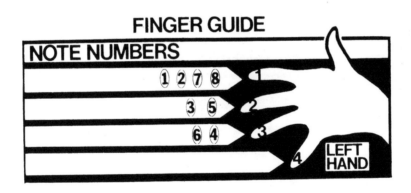

Student Notes

Photo Chart

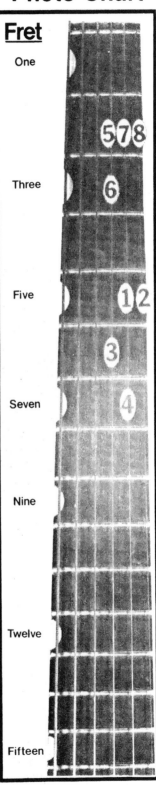

Bending Double Notes

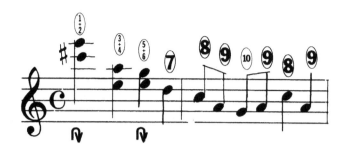

Special Instructions

To bend double notes, push notes ⑤ **and** ⑥ up at the same time.

Counting Review

Notes ⑤ **and** ⑥ are **quarter notes** and therefore receive only **one beat.** To bend both these notes and then also play **note** ⑦ in one beat will take time and practice.

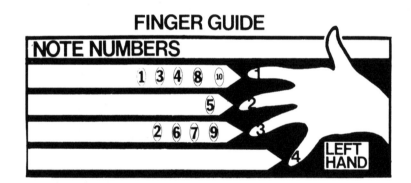

Complete Leads

Up to this point you have been given leads to demonstrate various techniques for playing lead guitar. In the next section of the book you will be given complete leads using all the techniques you have just learned. The leads have been broken into parts to make learning them easier. You should **learn each part before proceeding** to the **next part.** Once you have mastered each part you should combine all the parts into one complete lead.

Photo Chart

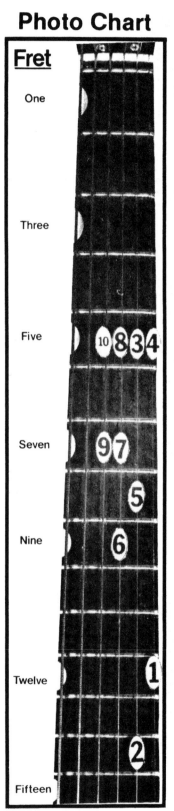

COMPLETE LEAD — NUMBER ONE

Photo Chart

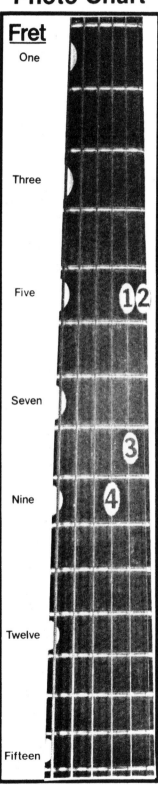

Below is Part I of your first complete lead. Remember to master each part before you proceed to the next. Once you have mastered each part you should be able to combine all the parts into a complete lead. When you play **all the parts of the lead,** they **should** all **flow together.** In other words, Part II should be played immediately after Part I.

Part I

Special Instructions

The first set of double notes must flow into the second set of double notes.

Counting

All the **double notes** are **eighth notes** so this part of the lead should take sixteen beats. (Refer to Counting Guide P. 7.)

FINGER GUIDE

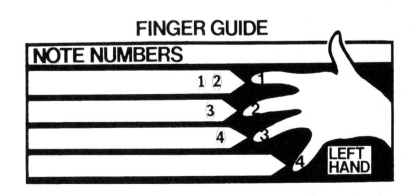

COMPLETE LEAD — NUMBER ONE

Part II

Photo Chart

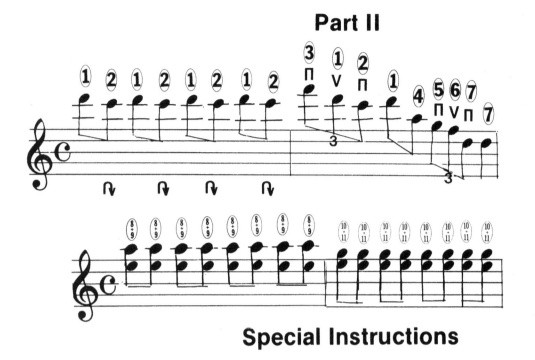

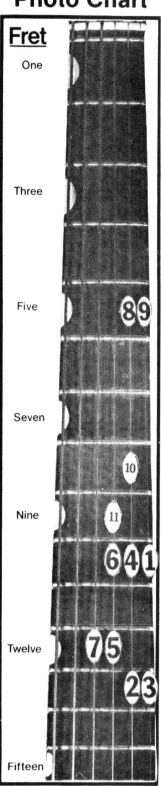

Special Instructions

Practice each part until there are no pauses.

Counting

Part II is also played in sixteen beats.

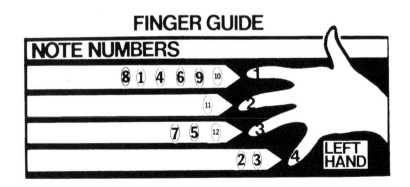

COMPLETE LEAD — NUMBER ONE

Part III

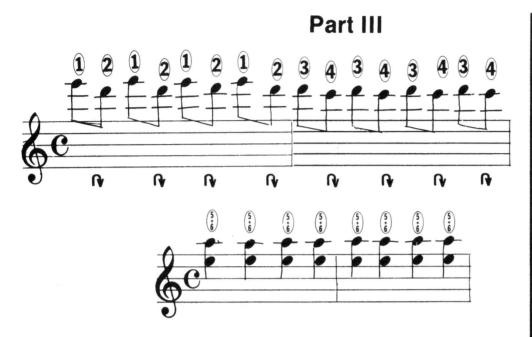

Photo Chart

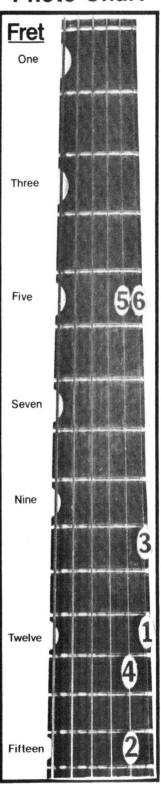

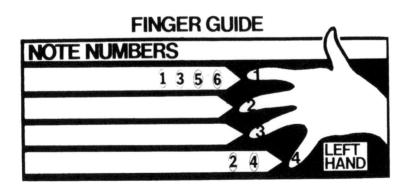

Special Instructions

You may notice that the last set of double notes are the same as those originally played in Part I.

FINGER GUIDE

COMPLETE LEAD — NUMBER ONE
(ALL PARTS)

For your convenience we have placed all three parts of the first complete lead on this page.

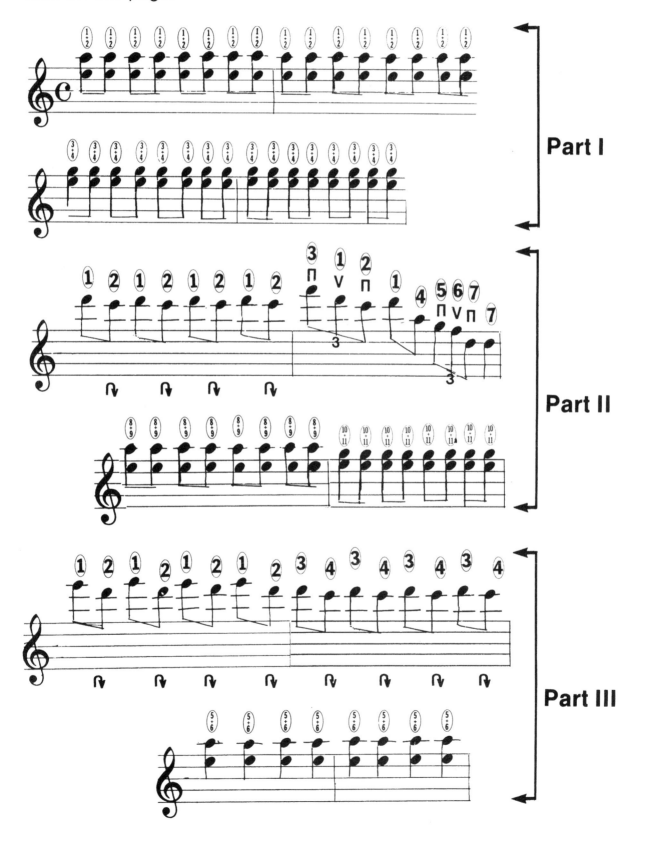

COMPLETE LEAD (PHOTO CHARTS)

For your convenience we have placed the Photo Charts for the three parts of your lead on this page.

Part I

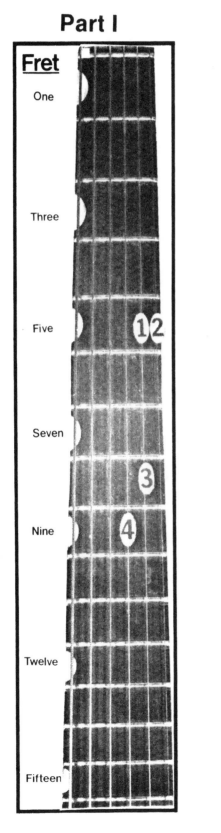

Part II

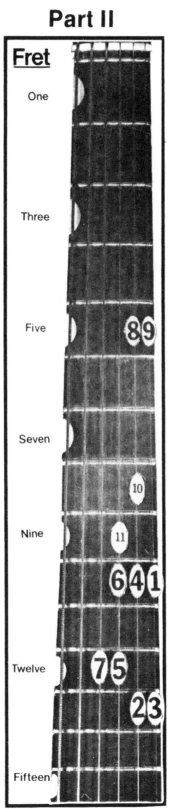

Part III

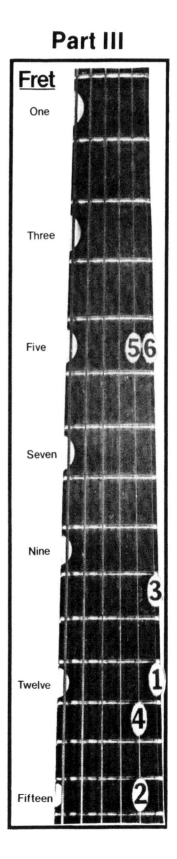

COMPLETE LEAD — NUMBER TWO

Part I

Photo Chart

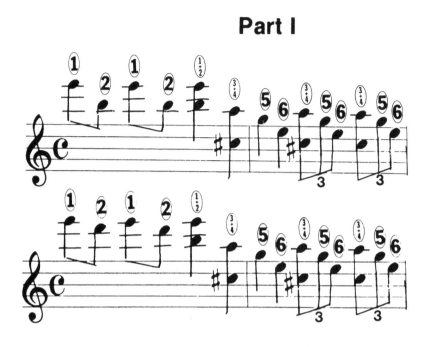

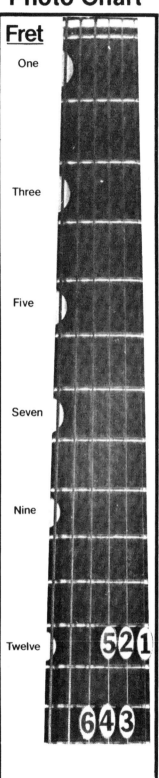

Special Instructions

Note that both lines of Part I of this lead are the same. Both lines should be played in sixteen beats.

FINGER GUIDE

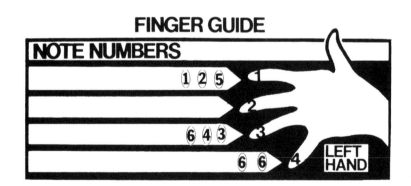

COMPLETE LEAD — NUMBER TWO

Part II

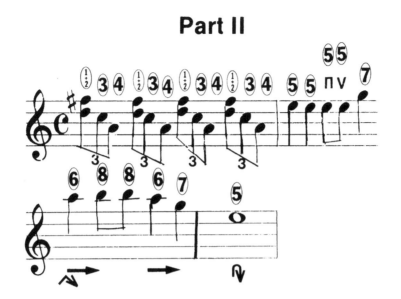

Special Instructions

Try to get from the first part to the second part as quickly as possible.

FINGER GUIDE

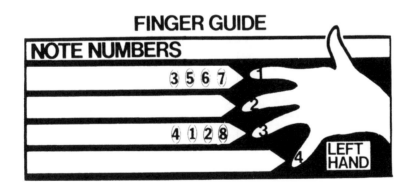

Photo Chart

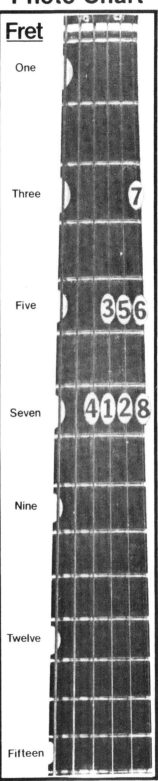

COMPLETE LEAD — NUMBER TWO

Part III

Photo Chart

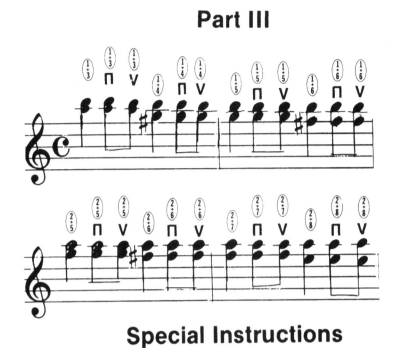

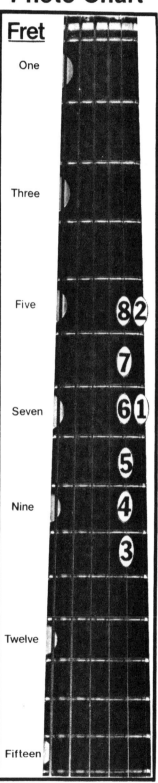

Special Instructions

You may have to practice the stretch from **note 1** to **note 3** and from **note 2** to **note 5**.

FINGER GUIDE

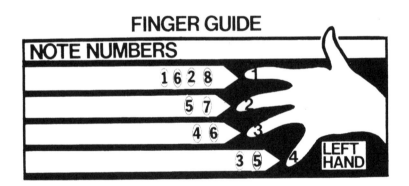

COMPLETE LEAD — NUMBER TWO

Part IV

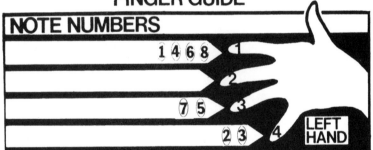

FINGER GUIDE

NOTE NUMBERS

LEFT HAND

Student Notes

Photo Chart

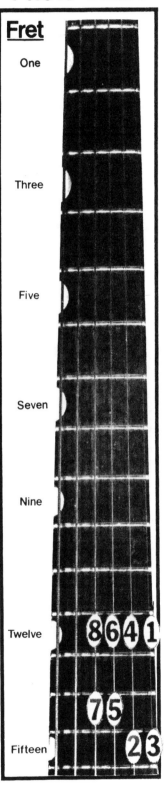

COMPLETE LEAD — NUMBER TWO
(ALL PARTS)

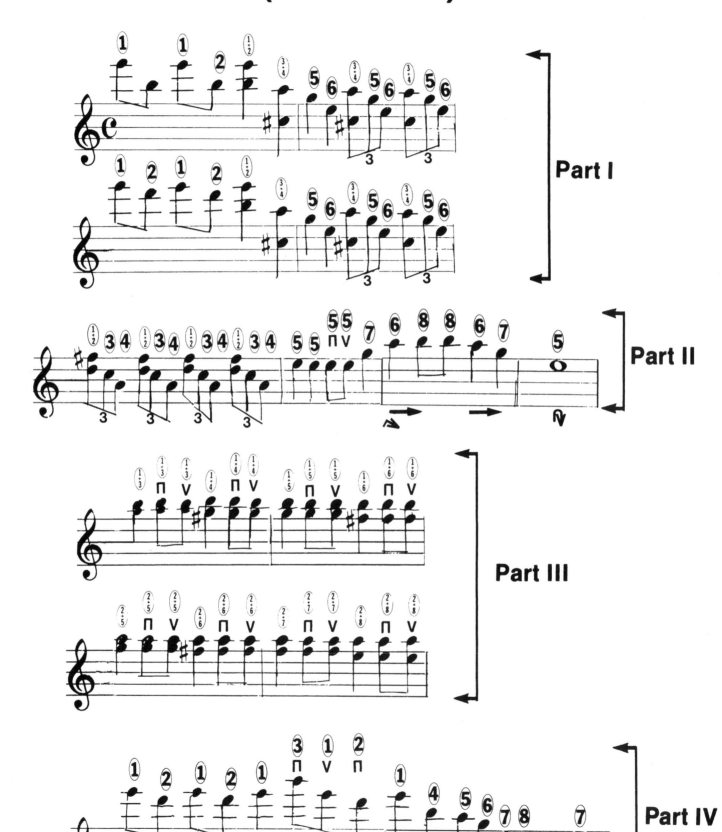

COMPLETE LEAD — NUMBER TWO
(ALL PARTS)

Part I   **Part II**   **Part III**   **Part IV**

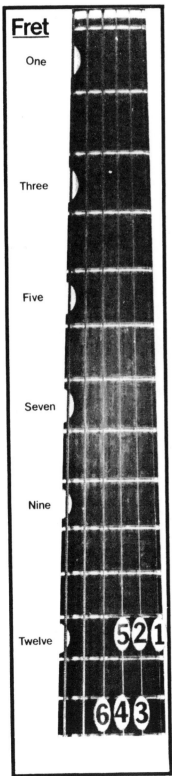
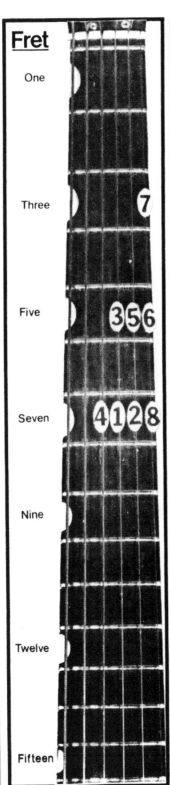
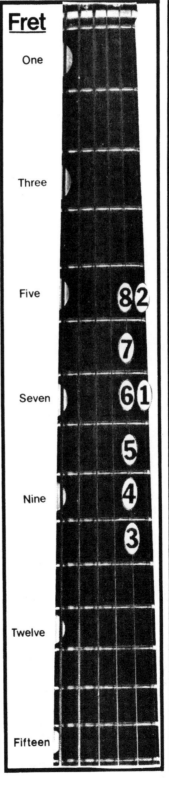
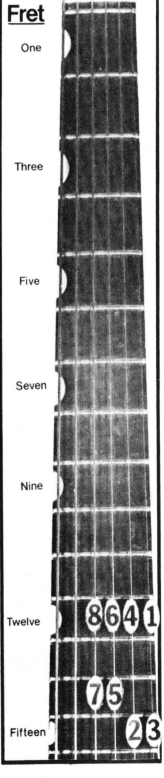

WRITE YOUR OWN LEADS

With the guitar diagrams below, you can diagram your own lead.

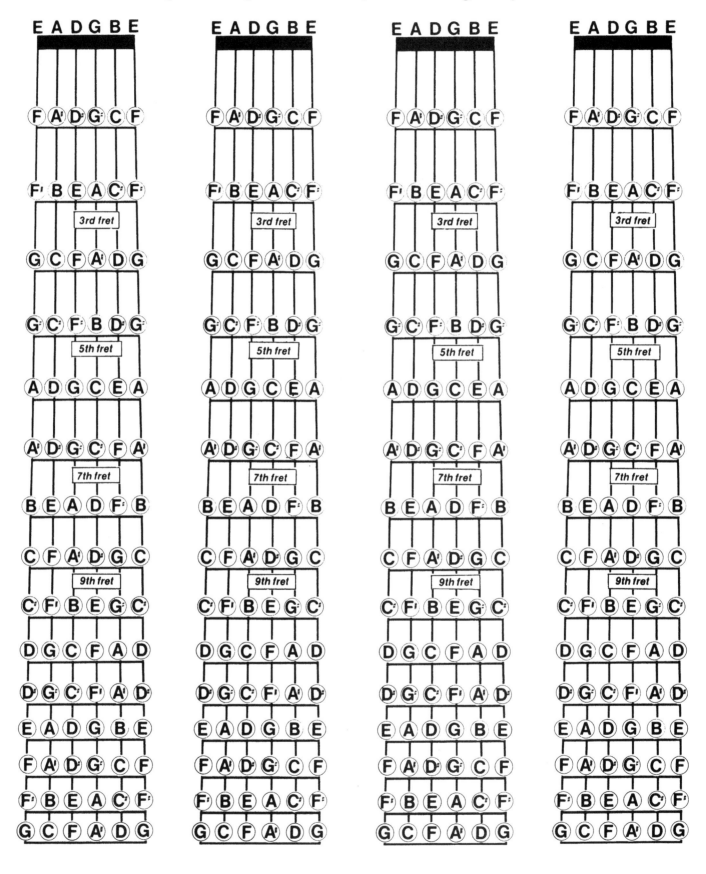

COMPLETE LEAD — NUMBER THREE

Part I

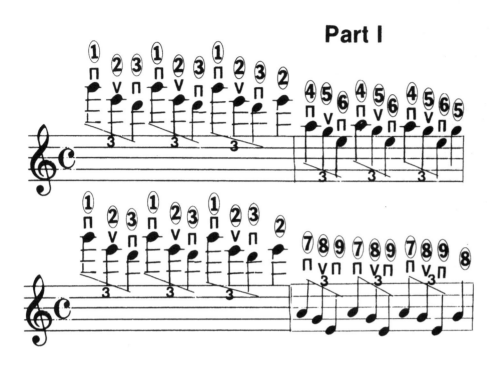

Photo Chart

Special Instructions

This is a great lead for you to use to practice double picking. Basically the same finger movement is being used on different places on the neck of the guitar.

FINGER GUIDE

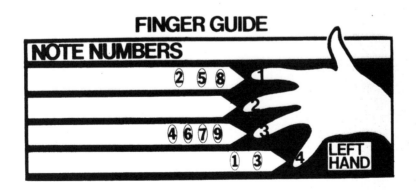

COMPLETE LEAD — NUMBER THREE

Part II

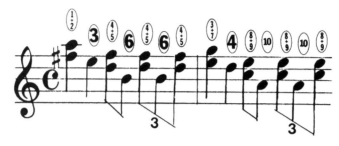

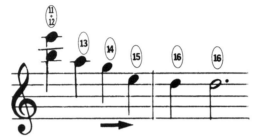

Photo Chart

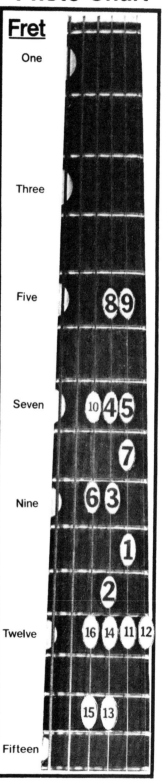

FINGER GUIDE

Student Notes

COMPLETE LEAD — NUMBER THREE

Part III

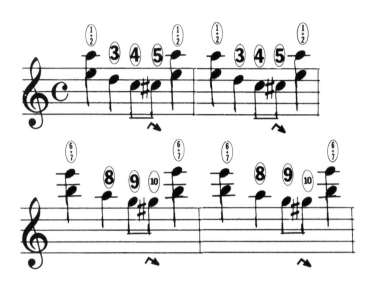

FINGER GUIDE

Photo Chart

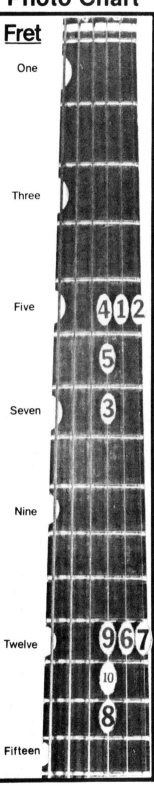

Student Notes

COMPLETE LEAD — NUMBER THREE
(ALL PARTS)

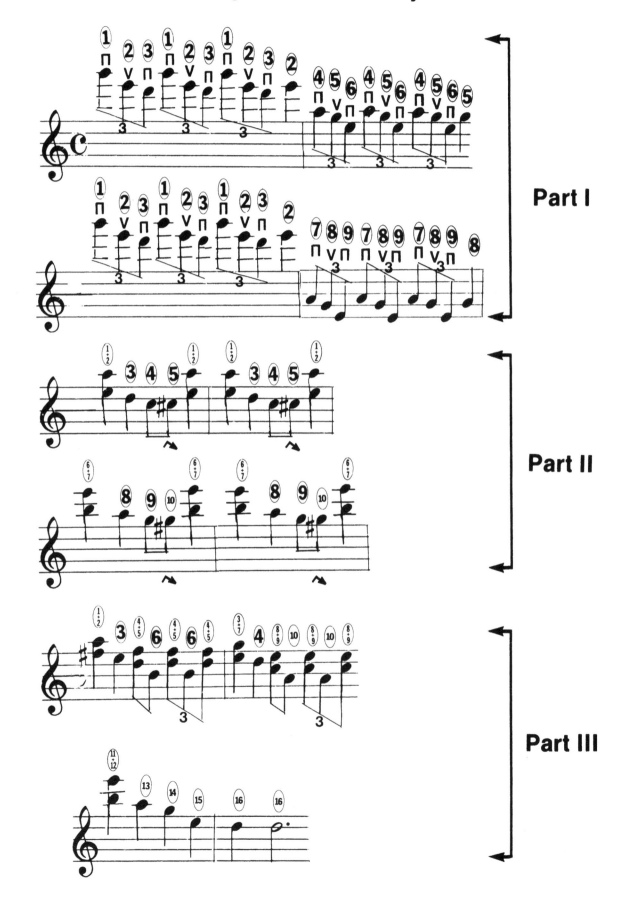

Part I

Part II

Part III

COMPLETE LEAD — NUMBER THREE
(ALL PARTS)

Part I

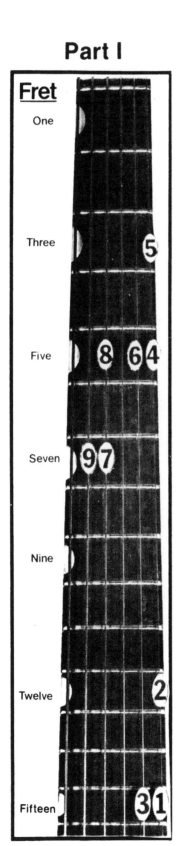

Part II

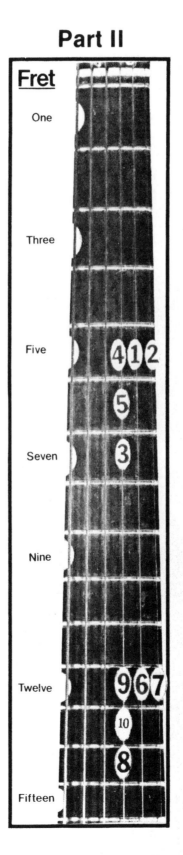

Part III

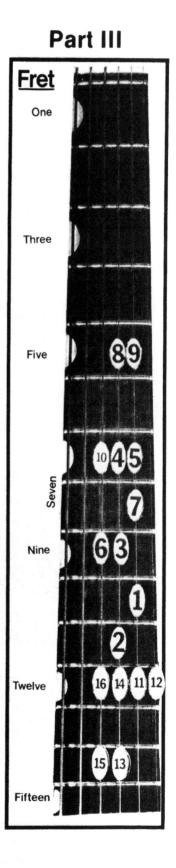

NOTE AND GUITAR POSITION GUIDE FOR FRETS 1-15

1. The word OPEN means that you play that string without putting any fingers of your left hand down on the neck of the guitar.

2. # is a sharp sign. b is a flat sign.

3. You will notice that often the same string and fret position is given two different names. For example, **string 1, fret 2** is called **F#** or **G b.** Since **F#** and **G b** are the **same note**, you may use either note or name to represent that position. The same holds true for all notes that are represented by two notes and two names.

4. This guide will help you find the position of notes you do not know or that we have not covered in this book. You may also use this guide to help you write your own leads. In order to do this, simply **find the position of the notes to your lead** on this guide and then **write them down.**

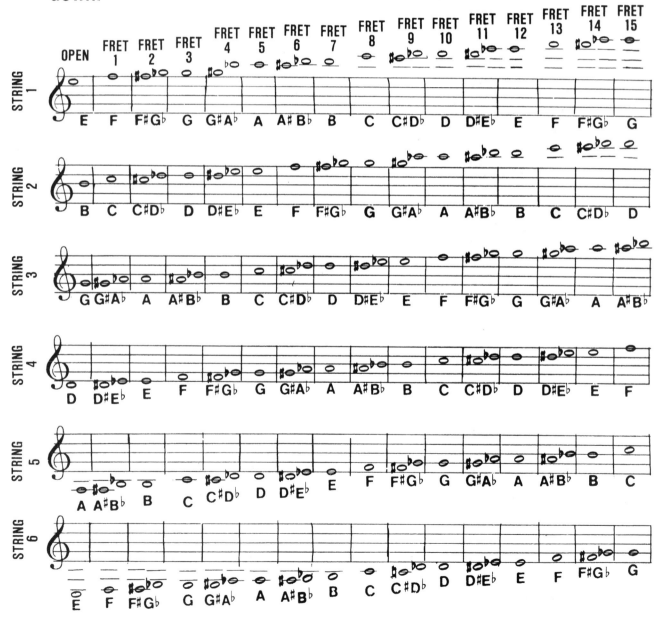